GOD IS ABLE

CONTENTS

Rise

Words and Music by
JOEL HOUSTON

PIANO · VOCAL · GUITAR

HILLSONG LIVE *God is able*

ISBN 978-1-4584-1204-1

7777 W. BLUEMOUND RD. P.O. BOX 13819 MILWAUKEE, WI 53213

Visit Hal Leonard Online at
www.halleonard.com

life - blood that nev - er ___ fails. ___ Your love, ___ it will nev - er fail. __
cross for __ our sin and __ shame. __ Our God, __ You will nev - er fail. __

VERSE 3

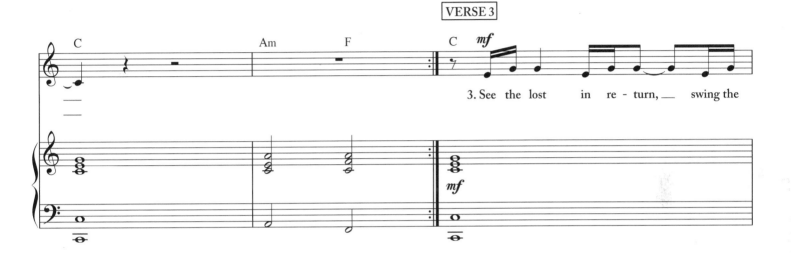

3. See the lost in re - turn, ___ swing the

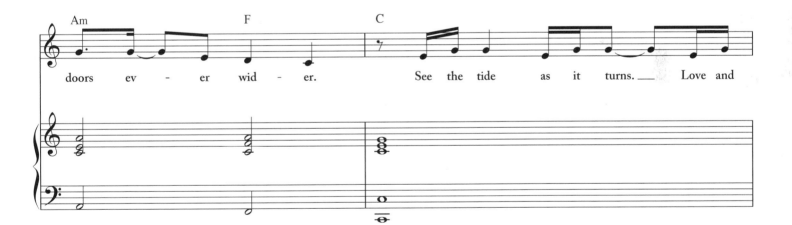

doors ev - er wid - er. See the tide as it turns. ___ Love and

mer - cy ___ is on the ___ rise, ___ as the world ___ folds in - to ___ Your light. __

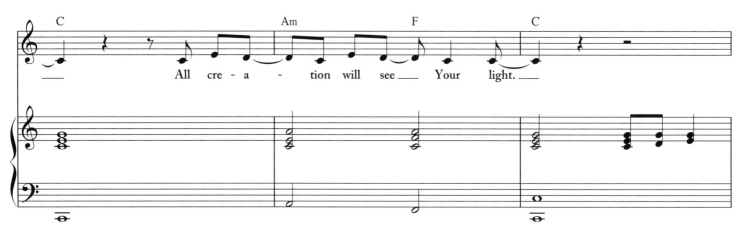

All cre - a - tion will see ___ Your light. ___

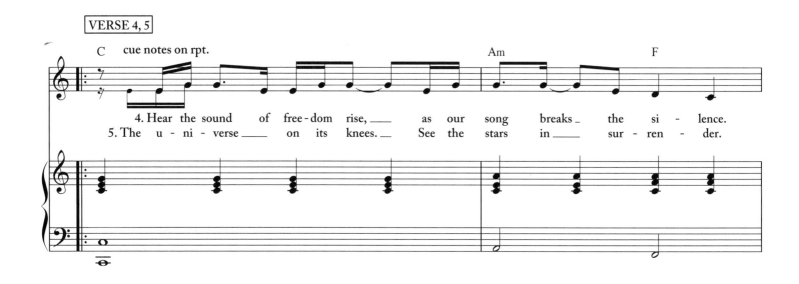

VERSE 4, 5

cue notes on rpt.

4. Hear the sound of free - dom rise, ___ as our song breaks ___ the si - lence.
5. The u - ni - verse ___ on its knees. ___ See the stars in ___ sur - ren - der.

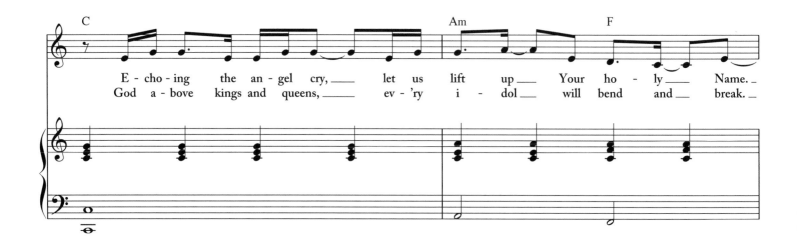

E - cho - ing the an - gel cry, ___ let us lift up ___ Your ho - ly ___ Name. ___
God a - bove kings and queens, ___ ev - 'ry i - dol ___ will bend and ___ break. ___

- er we'll lift ___ up ___ Your Name. ___

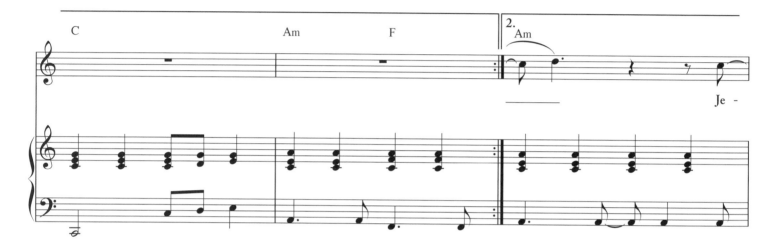

- sus. Je - sus. We will hold, we will love. ___ We will fall in sur - ren - der. ___

We will rise, we will run. ___ We will live to ___ de - clare Your ___ Name. ___ For - ev -

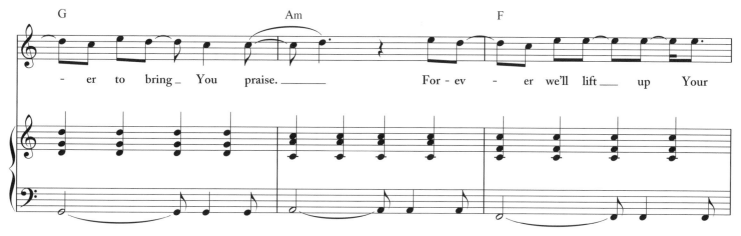

-er to bring __ You praise. _____ For - ev - er we'll lift __ up Your

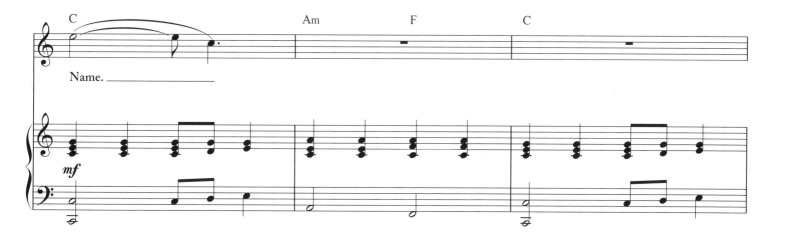

Name. _____

BRIDGE 1

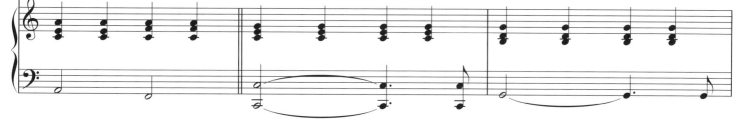

Swing __ the doors wid - er. Sound __ the praise loud - er.

All __ our hearts cry out for the glo - ry of Your __ Name. Our God, __

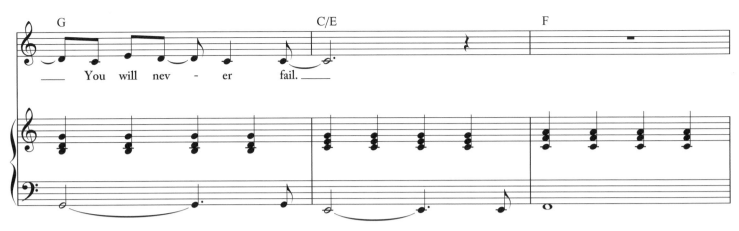

You will nev - er fail.

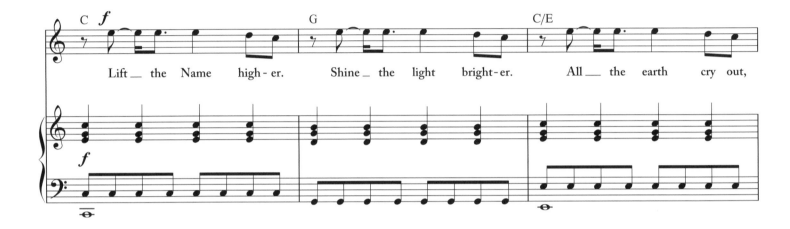

Lift _ the Name high-er. Shine _ the light bright-er. All _ the earth cry out,

for the glo - ry of Your _ Name. Our God, _ You will nev - er fail. _

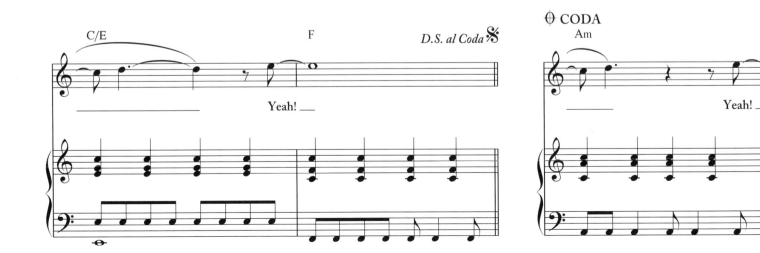

C/E F *D.S. al Coda* 𝄋 ⊕ CODA Am

_ Yeah! _ Yeah! _

BRIDGE 2

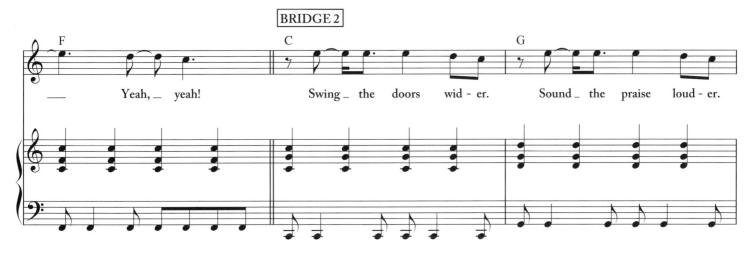

Yeah, __ yeah! Swing __ the doors wid - er. Sound __ the praise loud - er.

All __ our hearts cry out for the glo - ry of Your __ Name. Our God, __

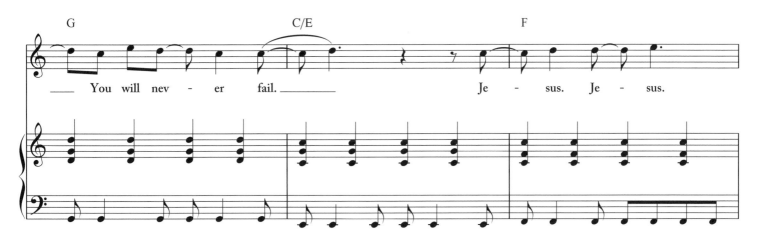

__ You will nev - er fail. _____ Je - sus. Je - sus.

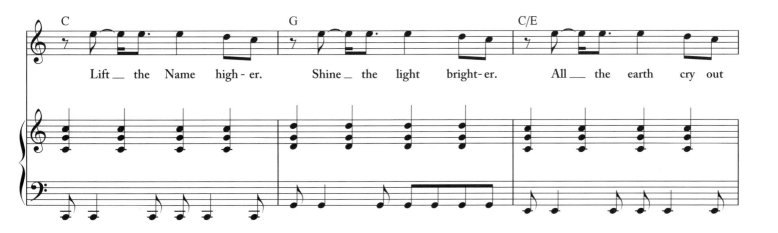

Lift __ the Name high - er. Shine __ the light bright - er. All __ the earth cry out

for the glo - ry of Your __ Name. Our God, __ You will nev - er fail.

__ For - ev - er __ we'll lift up __ Your Name. __

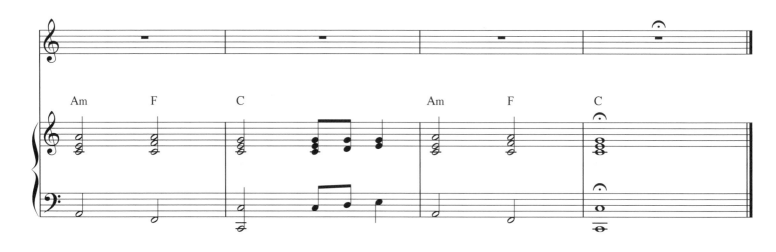

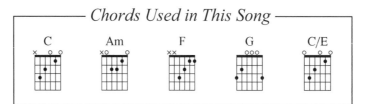

Chords Used in This Song

C   Am   F   G   C/E

With Us

Words and Music by REUBEN MORGAN
and DYLAN THOMAS

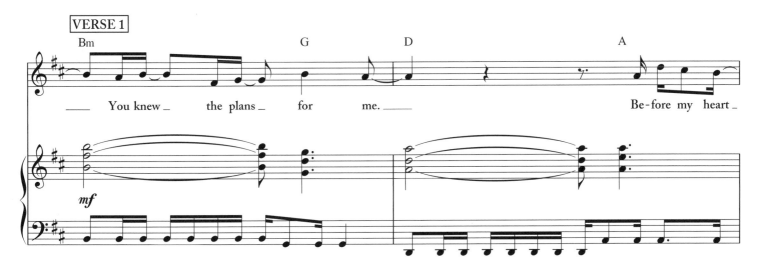

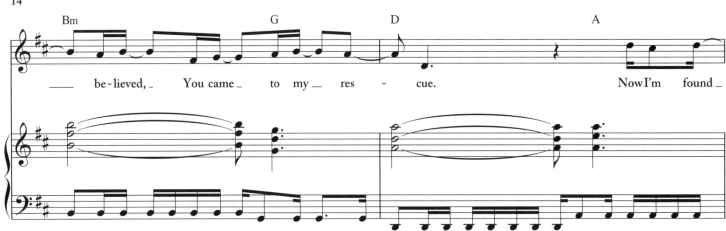

be-lieved, You came to my res - cue. Now I'm found

in love. There's no-where else to run. You keep my life

with - in Your might - y hands. Oh, God.

CHORUS 1

There's no end to Your love. There's no end to Your love.

You're with __ us. You're with __ us. There's noth-ing __ in this world

that could take __ You a-way. You're with __ us. You're with __ us.

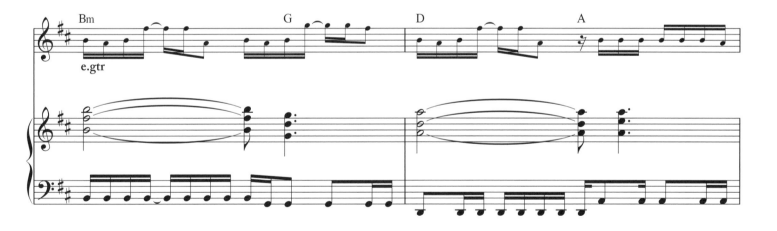

e.gtr

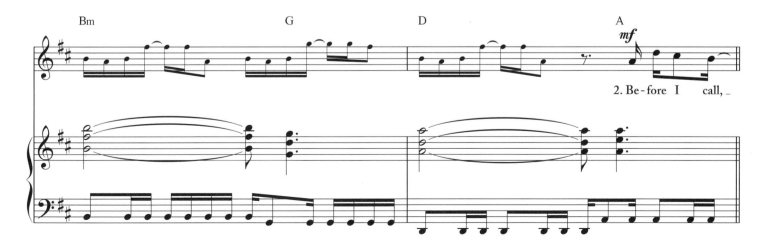

2. Be-fore I call, __

VERSE 2

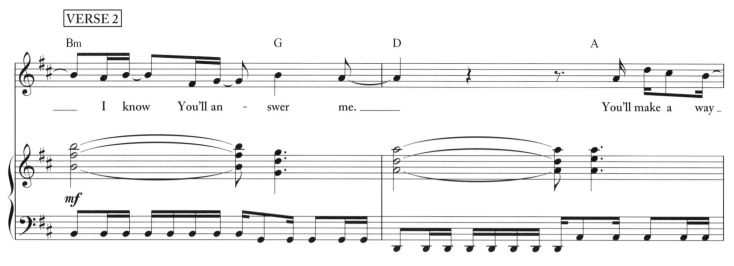

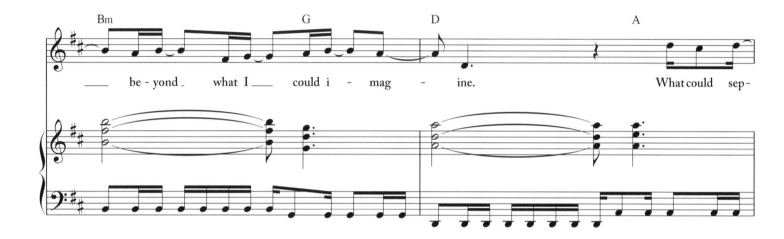

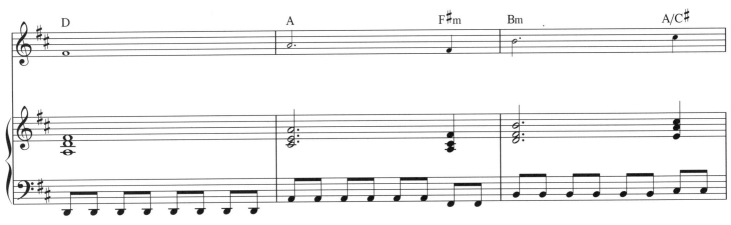

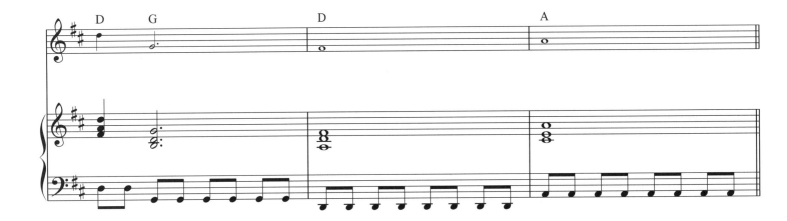

BRIDGE

You reign in our __ hearts. You reign a - bove __ all.

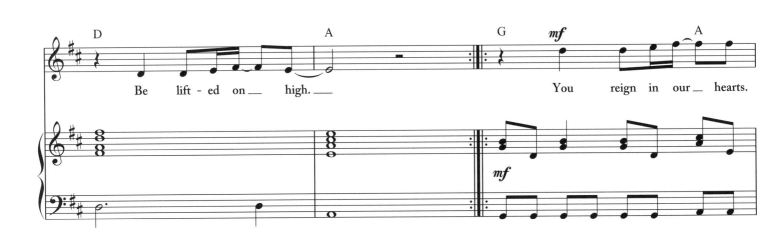

Be lift - ed on __ high. __ You reign in our __ hearts.

2nd time D.S. al Coda

You reign a-bove _ all. Be lift-ed on __ high. __

2nd time cresc.

⊕ CODA

e.gtr

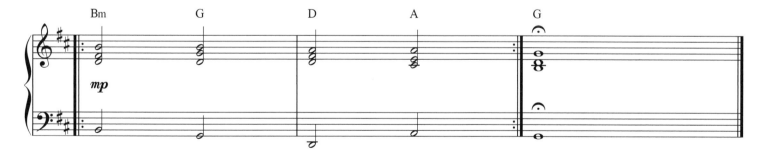

mp

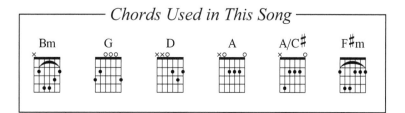

Chords Used in This Song

Bm   G   D   A   A/C♯   F♯m

Unending Love

Words and Music by SAM KNOCK
and JILL McCLOGHRY

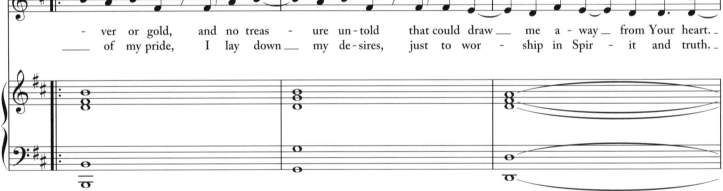

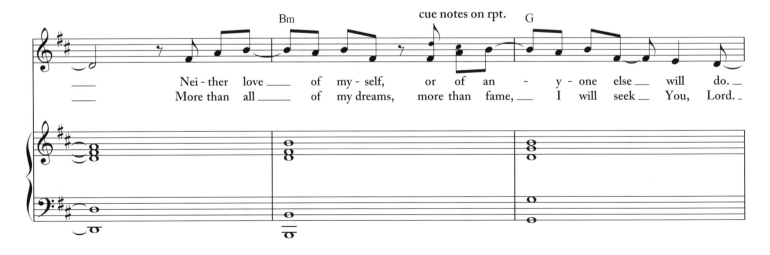

CHANNEL

I lay at Your feet. I'm hum-bled by the won-der of Your maj - es - ty.

One thing I know: I find all I need in Your un - end - ing love,

INSTRUMENTAL

in Your un - end - ing love.

CHANNEL

Je - sus, ___

n- oth - ing com - pares ___ to this grace ___ that res - cues me. ___

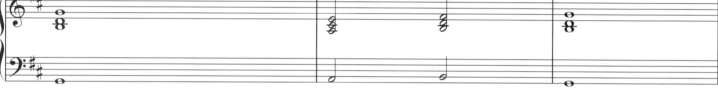

Sav - iour, ___ now and for - ev - er, Your face ___ is all ___ I seek.

1.

2.

D.S. al Coda 𝄋
(take 2nd ending)

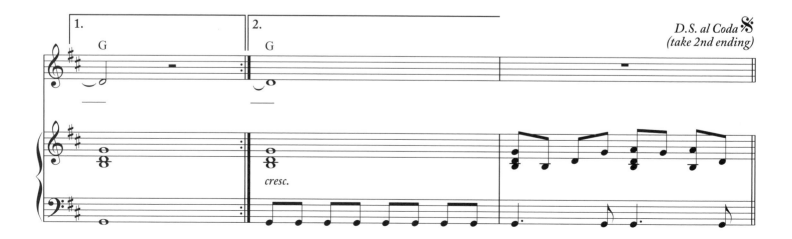

cresc.

Chords Used in This Song

The Lost Are Found

Words and Music by BEN FIELDING
and SAM KNOCK

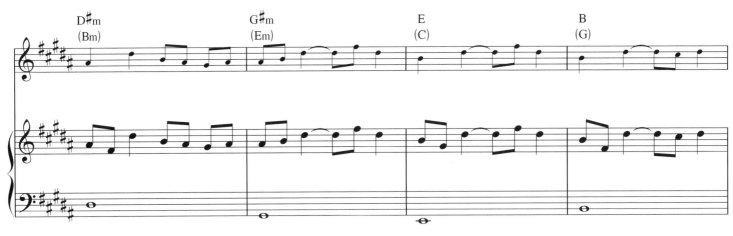

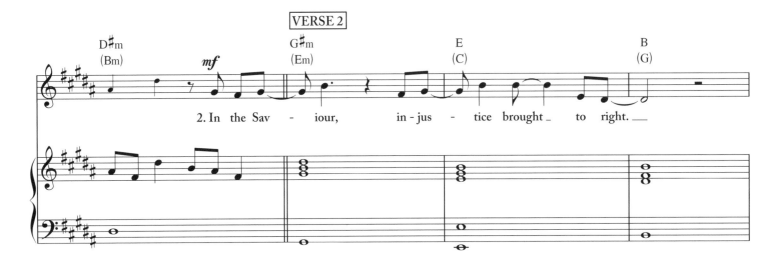

VERSE 2

2. In the Sav - iour, in - jus - tice brought to right.

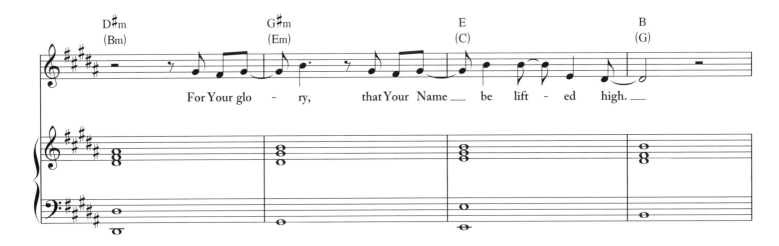

For Your glo - ry, that Your Name be lift - ed high.

CHORUS 2

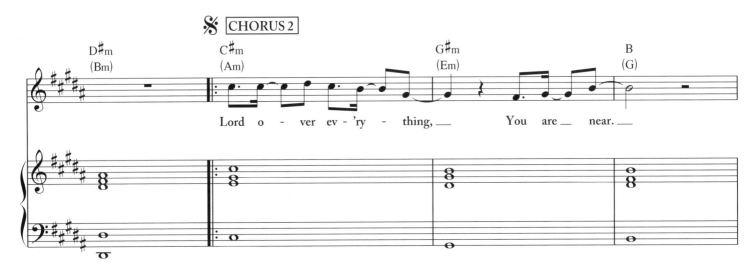

Lord o - ver ev - 'ry - thing, You are near.

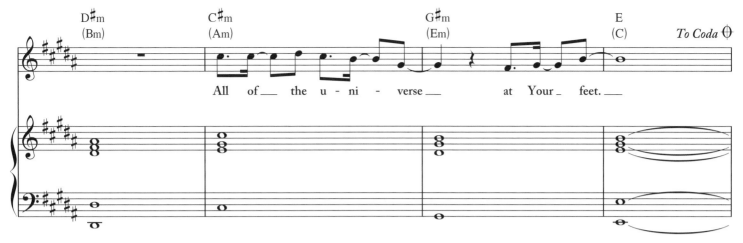

All of ___ the u - ni - verse ___ at Your _ feet. ___

INSTRUMENTAL 1

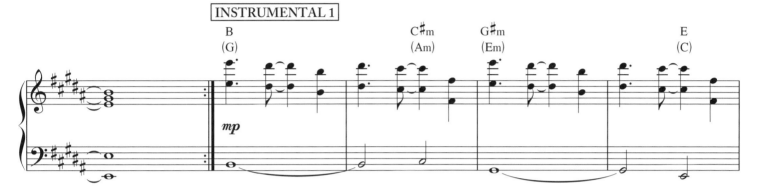

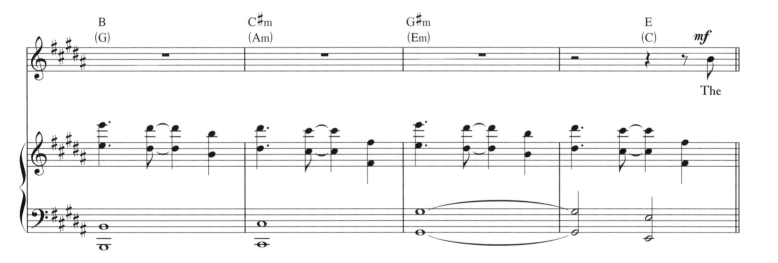

The

BRIDGE 1

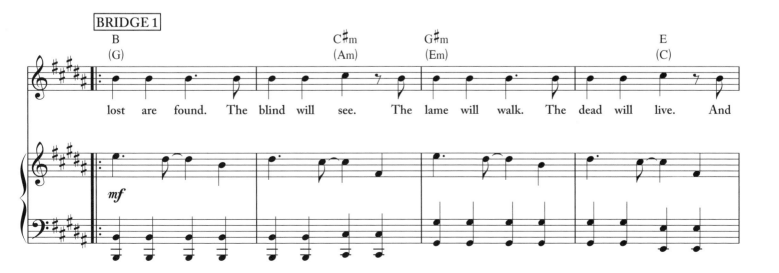

lost are found. The blind will see. The lame will walk. The dead will live. And

You, our God, for-ev-er You will reign._____ The

INSTRUMENTAL 2

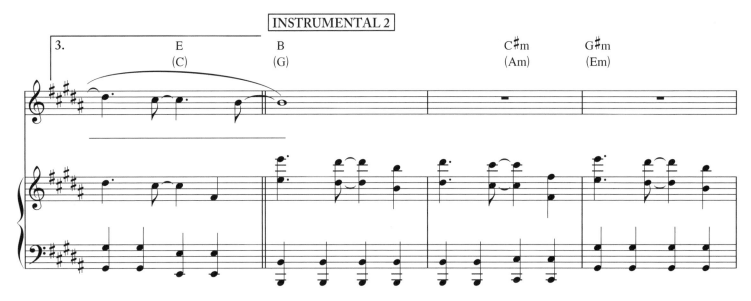

D.S. al Coda 𝄋   𝄌 CODA   **BRIDGE 2**

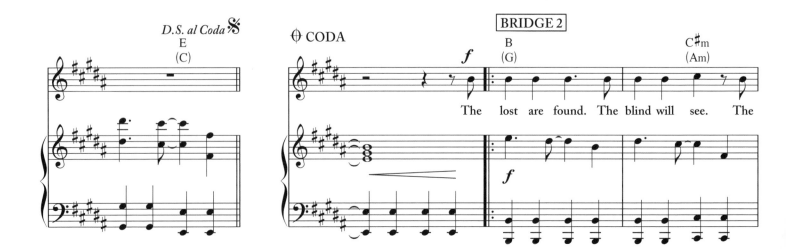

The lost are found. The blind will see. The

lame will walk. The dead will live. And You, our God, for - ev - er You will

reign. The

1.–3. E (C) **4.** E (C) B (G)

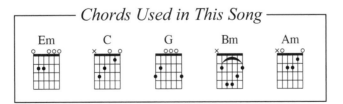

Chords Used in This Song

Em   C   G   Bm   Am

God Is Able

Words and Music by REUBEN MORGAN
and BEN FIELDING

Capo 4 (G)

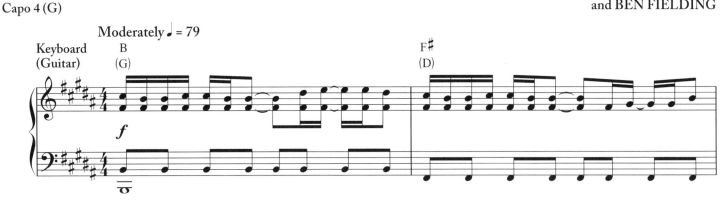

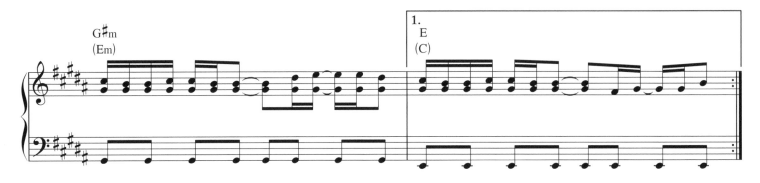

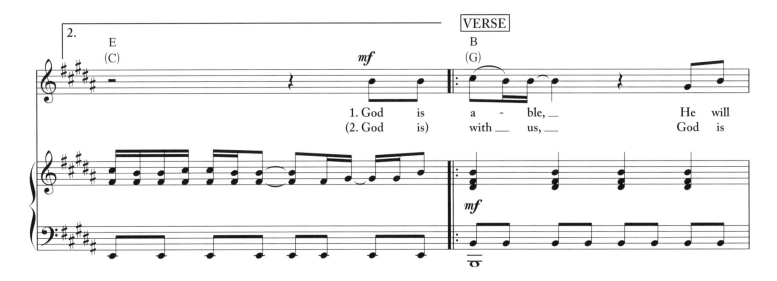

1. God is a - ble, He will never fail. He is Al - might - y God.
(2. God is) with us, God is on our side. He will make a way.

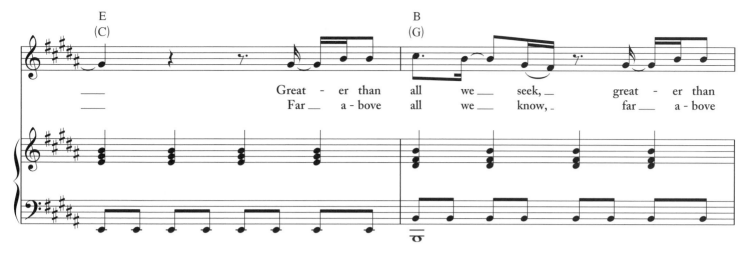

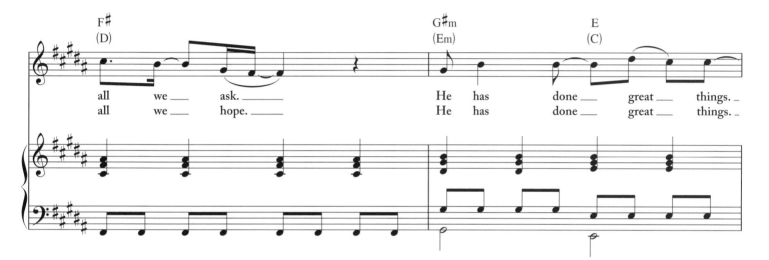

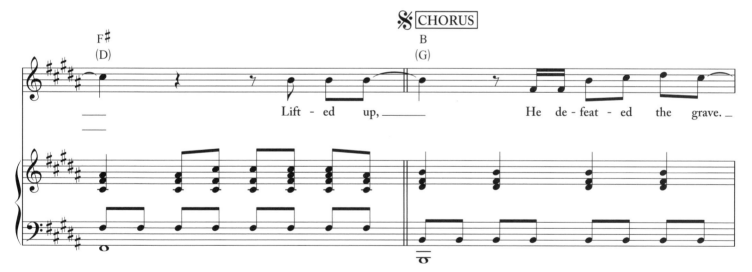

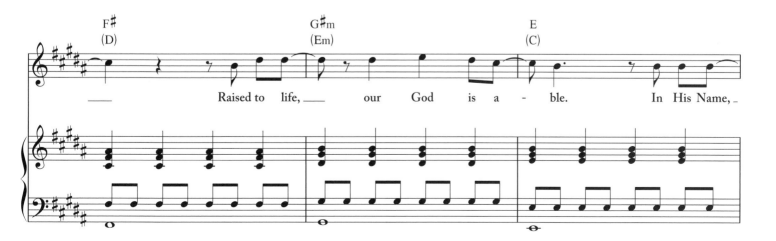

we o-ver-come, _____ for the Lord _____ our God is a-

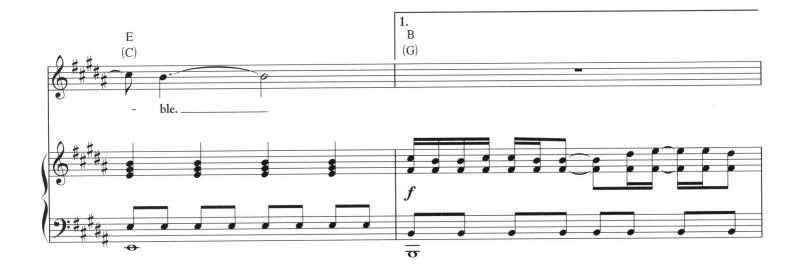

- ble. _____

2. God is

e.gtr

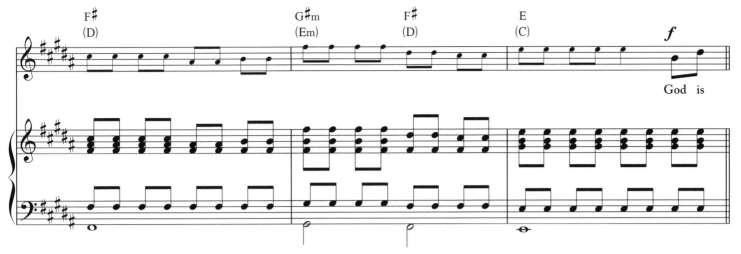

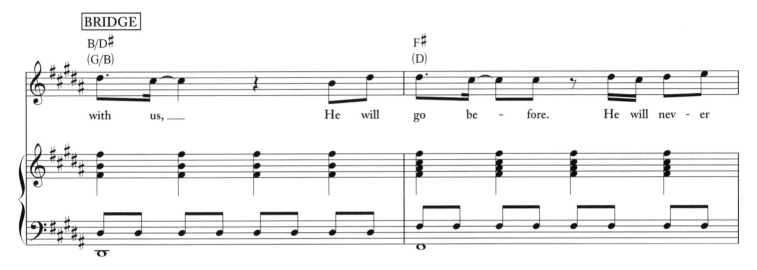

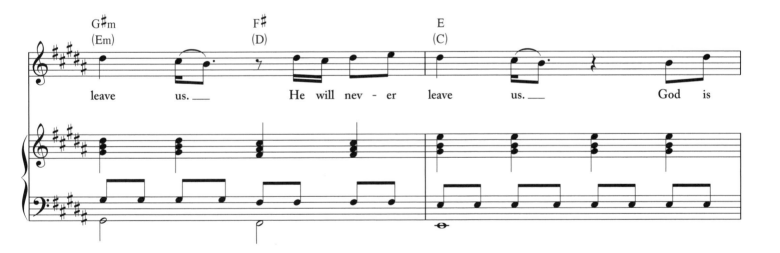

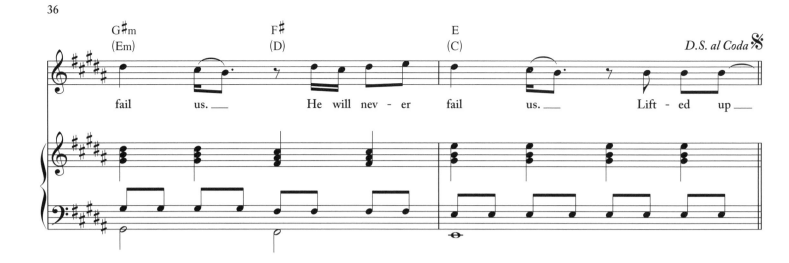

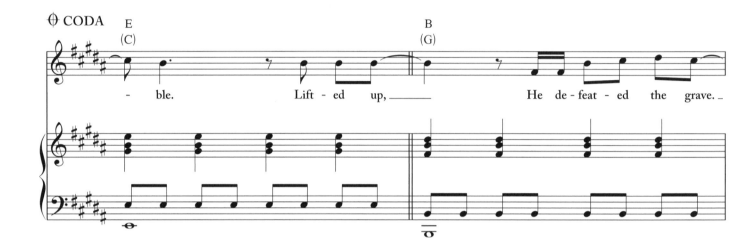

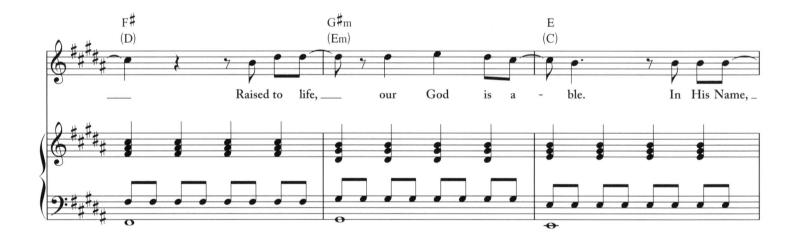

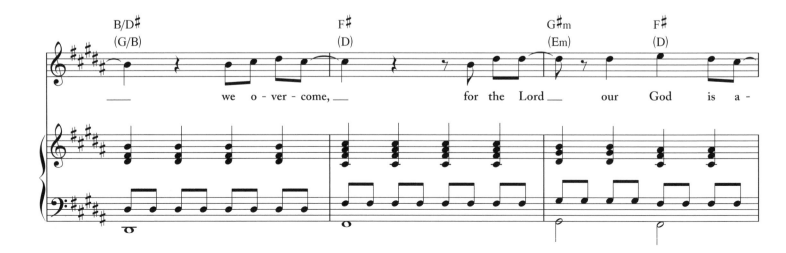

-ble. For the Lord ___ our God is a - ble. For the Lord ___

___ our God is a - ble. ___

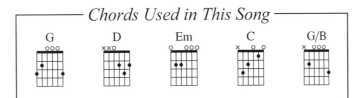

Chords Used in This Song

G   D   Em   C   G/B

The Difference

Words and Music by BEN FIELDING
and JOEL DAVIES

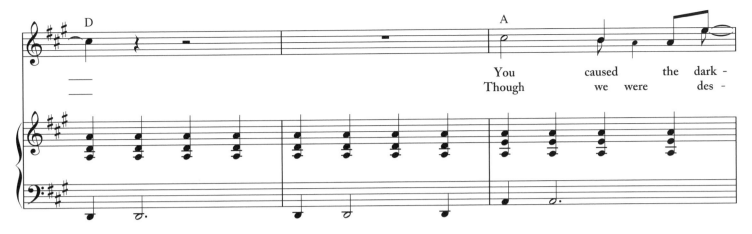

You caused the dark -
Though we were des -

- ness _____ to end. _____ You lift - ed _____ our heads _____
- tined _____ to fail, _____ You o - pened _____ the _ way _

_____ to know _ You _____ a - gain. _____
_____ and broke _ ev - 'ry chain. _____

Lord, You

CHANNEL

bring us to life. In You, our hope will a - rise.

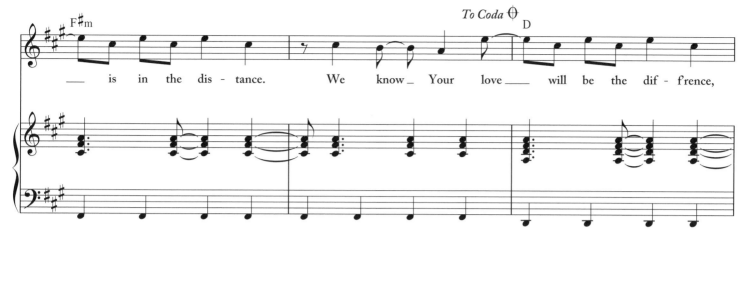

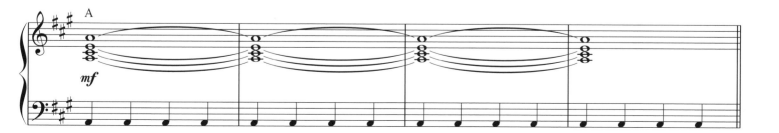

D.S. al Coda 𝄋

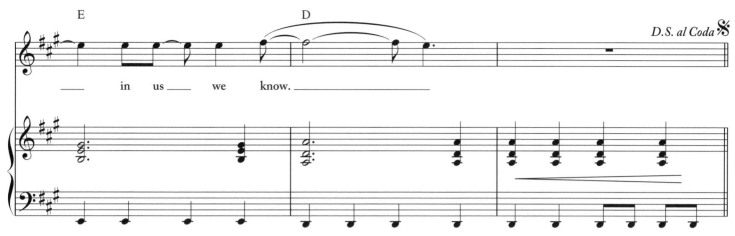

in us ___ we know. ___

𝄌 CODA

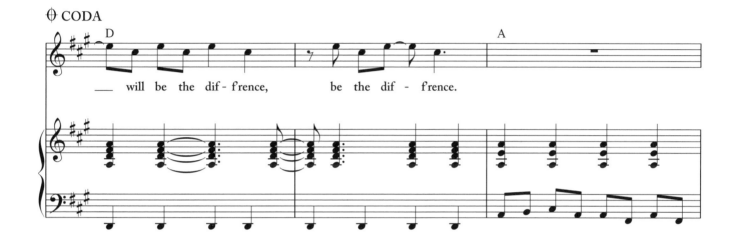

___ will be the dif - frence, be the dif - frence.

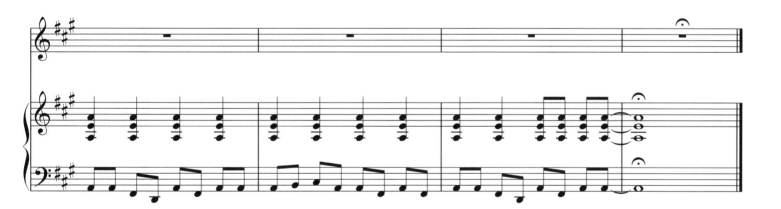

Chords Used in This Song

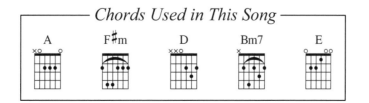

Alive in Us

Words and Music by JASON INGRAM
and REUBEN MORGAN

Moderate Rock ♩ = 85

solo gtr.

f

VERSE

mf

1. Great is Your love. Let the whole earth sing.
2. You out-shine the sun. You are glo-ri-ous.

mf

Let the whole earth sing.
You are glo-ri-ous.

You reached for us,
Lord o-ver all,

from on heav-en's __ throne, when we had no __ hope. __ You are the
You have made us __ new, we owe it all to __ You. __ In ev-'ry -

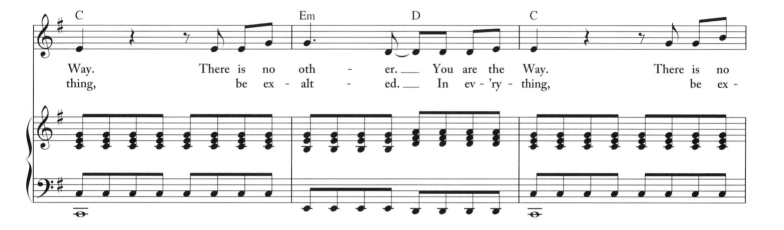

Way. There is no oth - er. __ You are the Way. There is no
thing, be ex - alt - ed. __ In ev-'ry - thing, be ex -

CHORUS

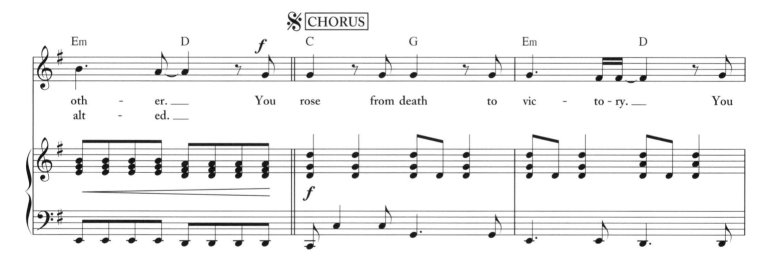

oth - er. __ You rose from death to vic - to-ry. __ You
alt - ed. __

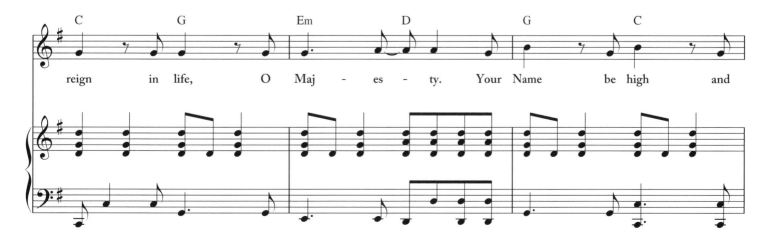

reign in life, O Maj - es - ty. Your Name be high and

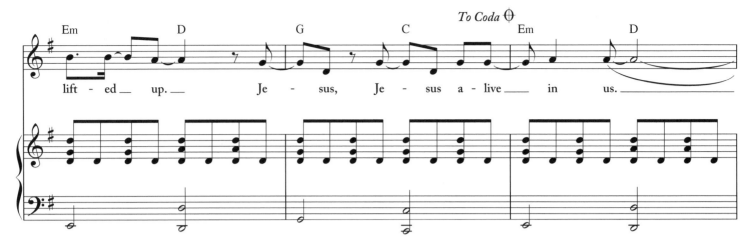

lift - ed __ up. __ Je - sus, Je - sus a - live __ in us. __

solo gtr.

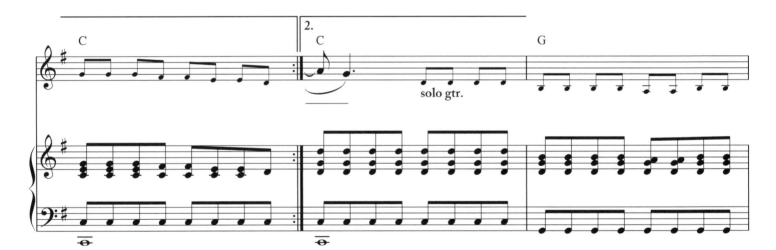

solo gtr.

BRIDGE

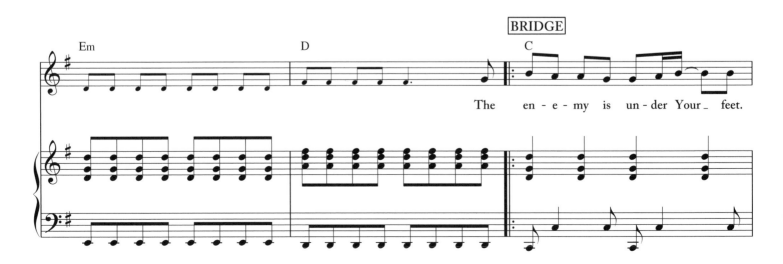

The en - e - my is un - der Your __ feet.

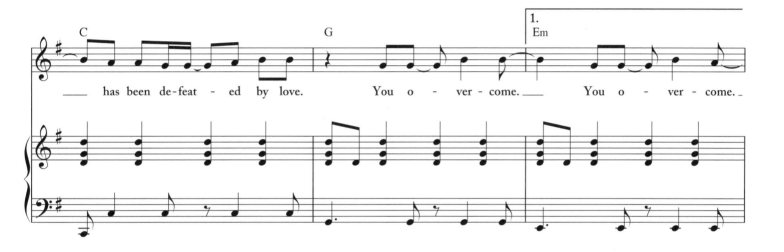

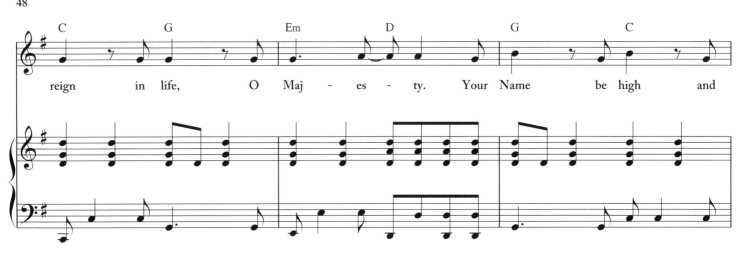

reign in life, O Maj - es - ty. Your Name be high and

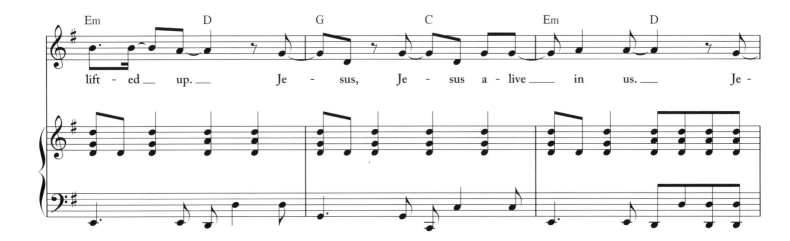

lift - ed __ up. __ Je - sus, Je - sus a - live __ in us. __ Je -

__ sus, Je - sus a - live __ in us. _____

rit.

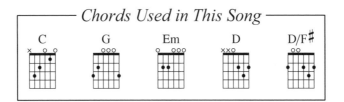

Chords Used in This Song

C   G   Em   D   D/F#

You Are More

Words and Music by
HARRISON WOOD

Capo 4 (G)

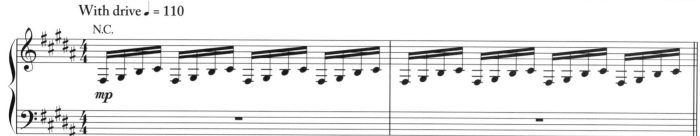

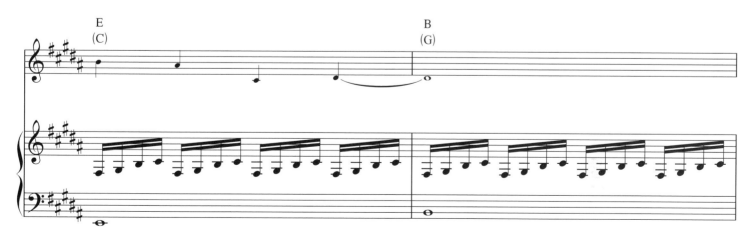

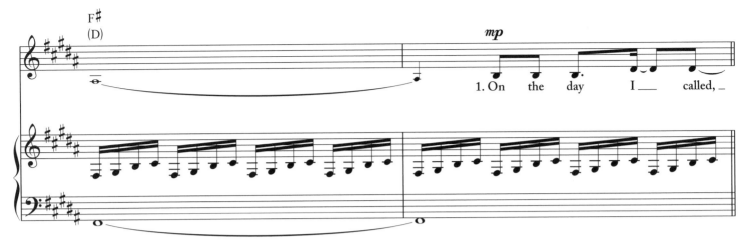

VERSE 1

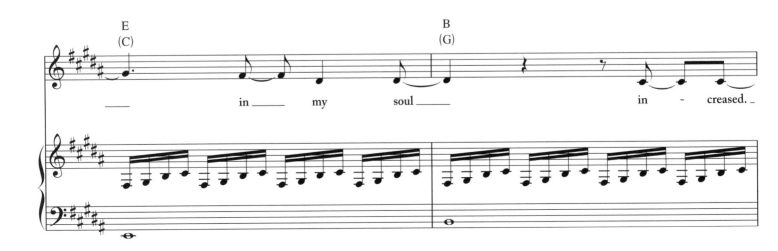

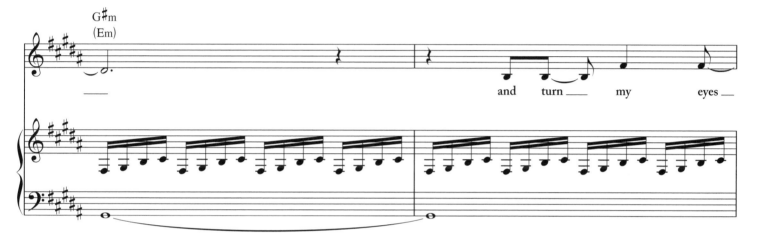

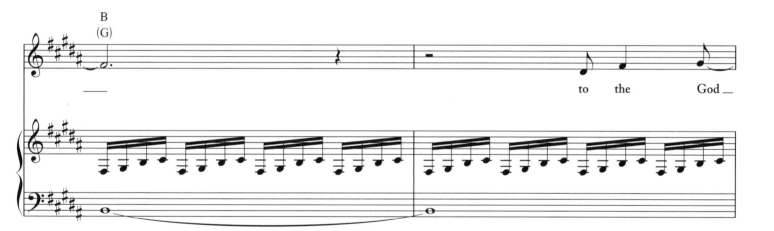

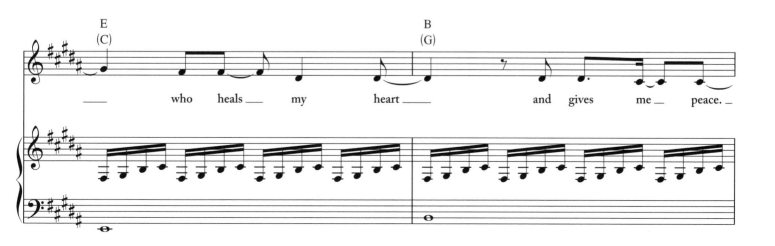

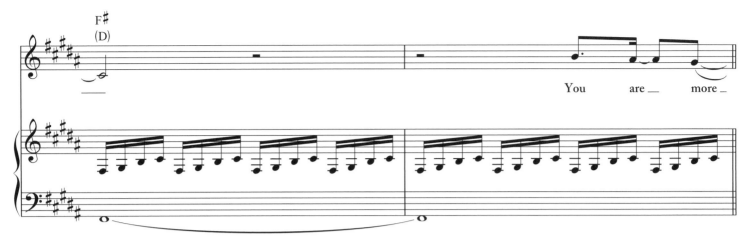

CHORUS 1

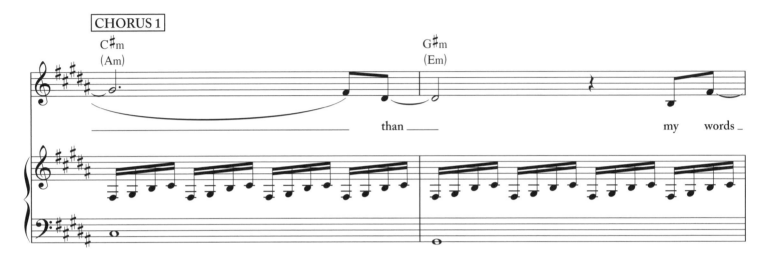

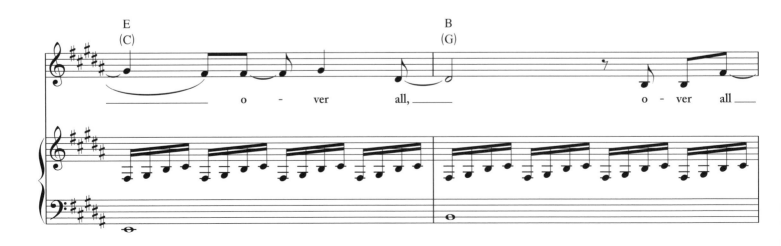

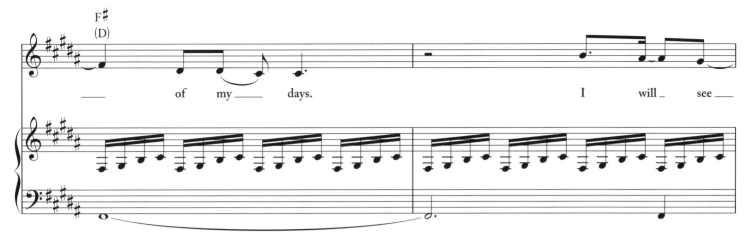

of my ____ days. I will ___ see ____

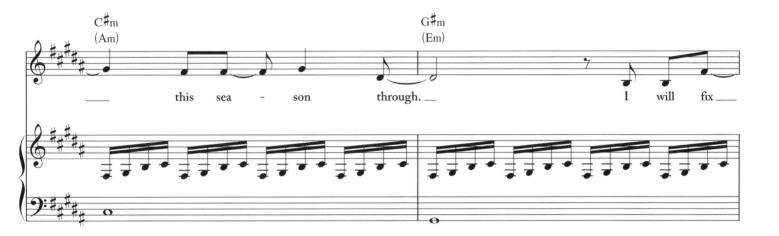

____ this sea - son through. ___ I will fix ____

____ my eyes ____ on You, ____ on - ly You, _

on - ly You. _

VERSE 2

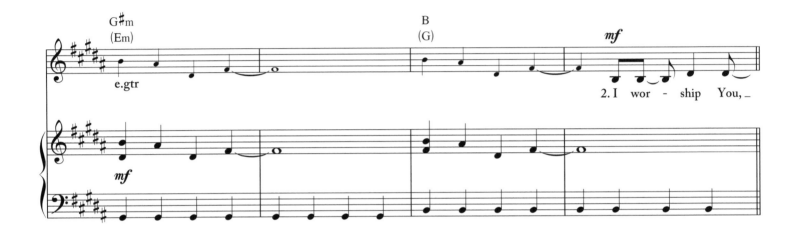

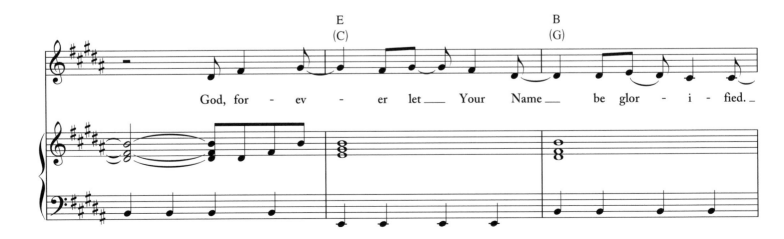

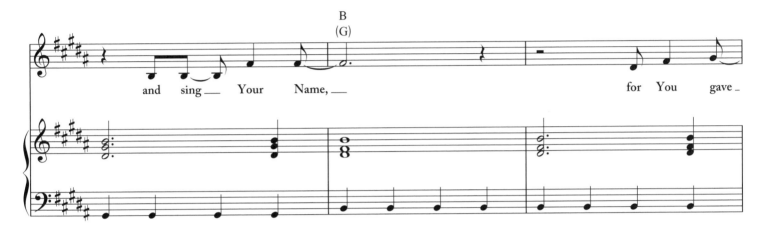

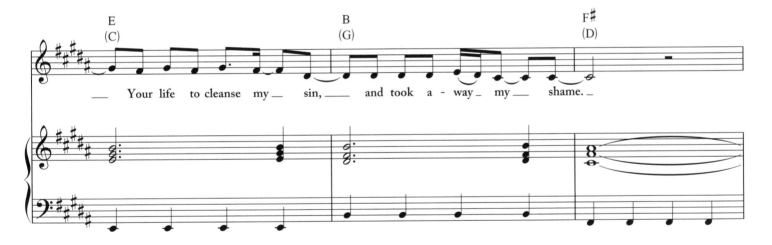

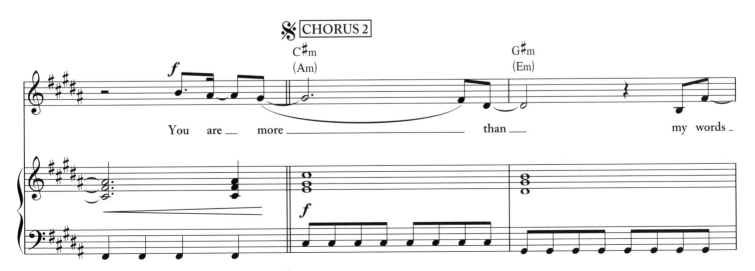

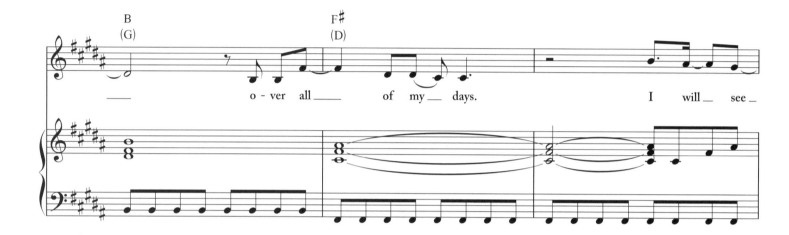

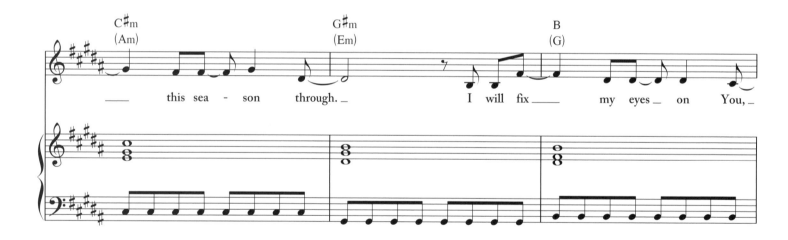

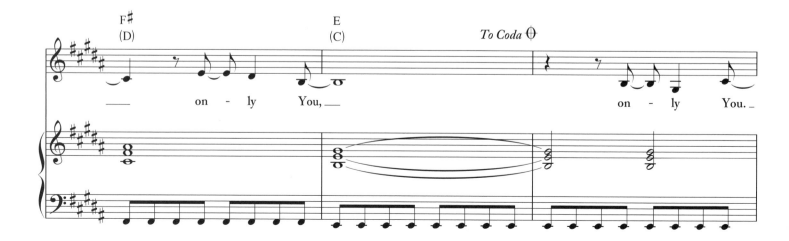

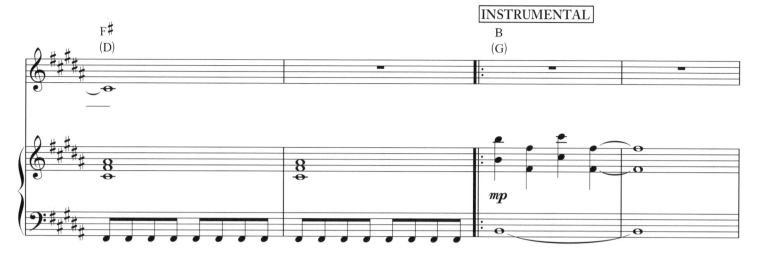

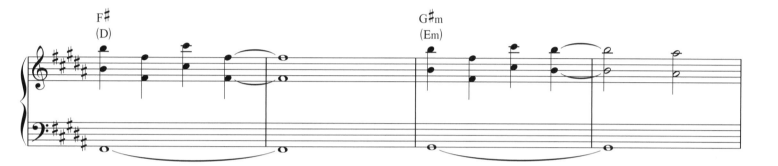

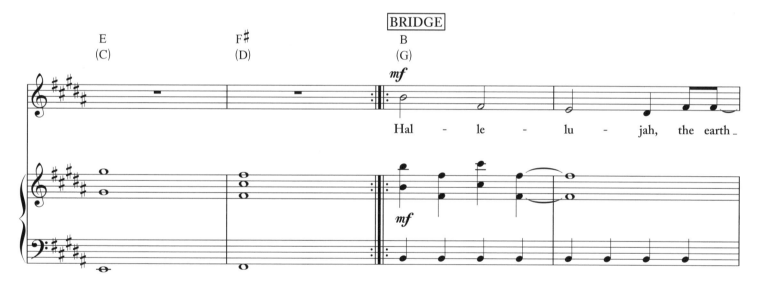

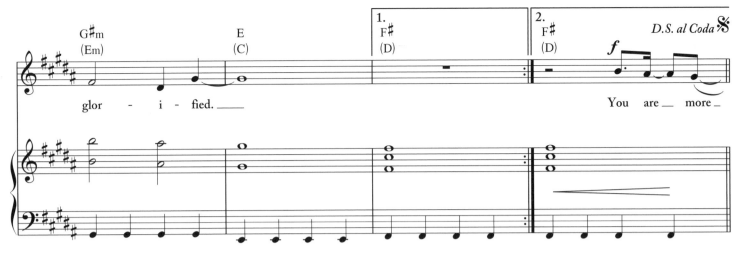

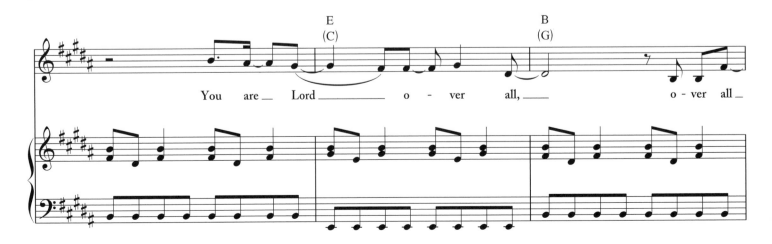

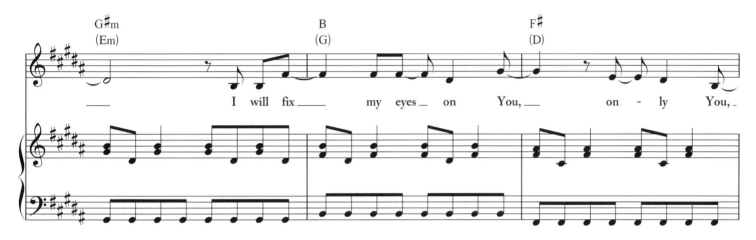

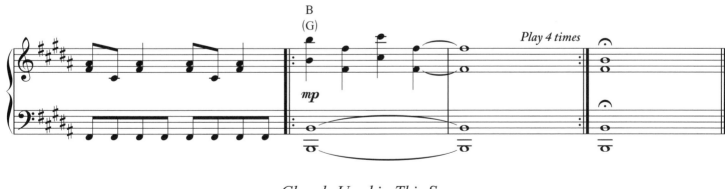

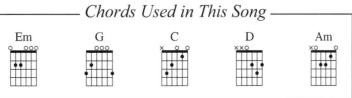

Narrow Road

Words and Music by
BRADEN LANG

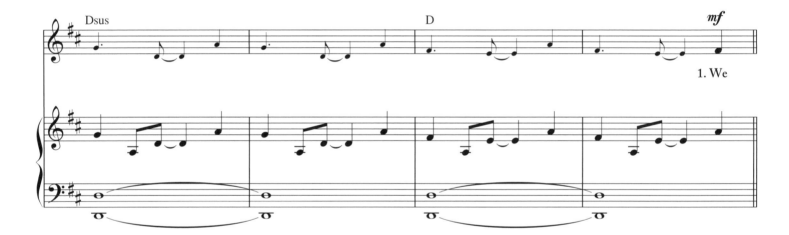

one we walk in Your __ hope. And
sin - ner's plight through Your __ love. Our

though dark - ness fills our path, fear won't fix its
eyes set up - on this task, truth in hand, as

hold on us, for we __ know. And
one we walk, we ad - vance.

CHANNEL

love will shine be - fore us on our __ path, and
(D.S.) to

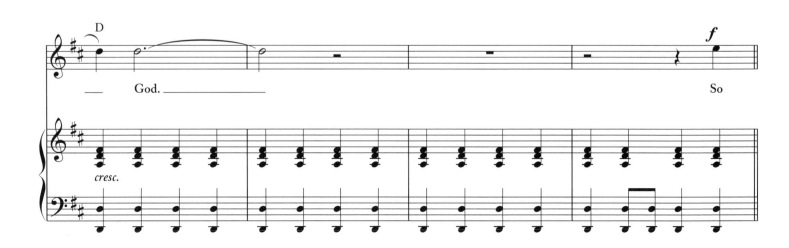

CHORUS

Lord, here we are __ with hum - bled hearts, to

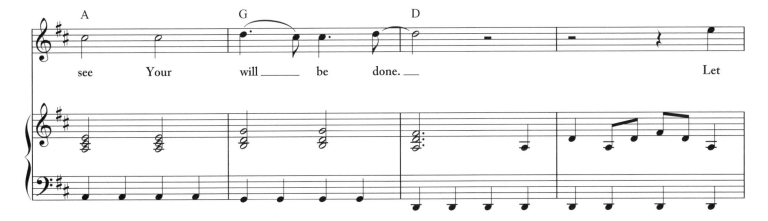

see Your will ___ be done. __ Let

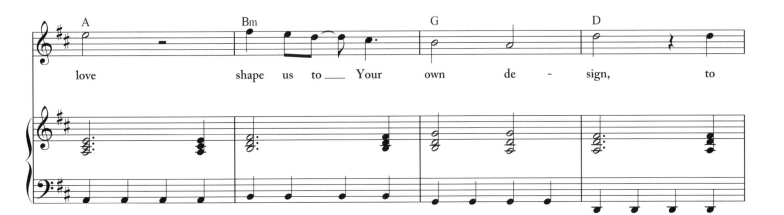

love shape us to __ Your own de - sign, to

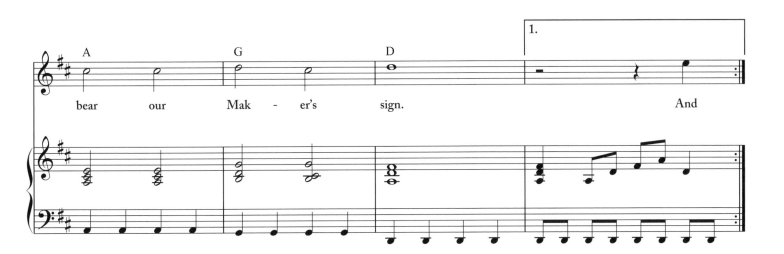

bear our Mak - er's sign. And

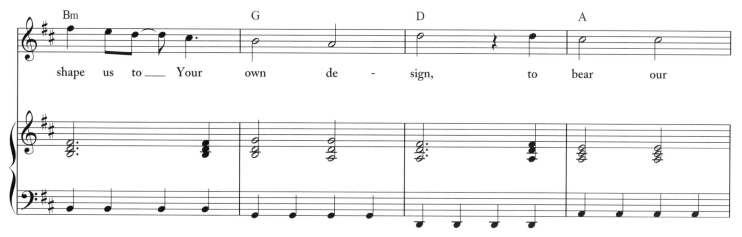

shape us to ___ Your own de - sign, to bear our

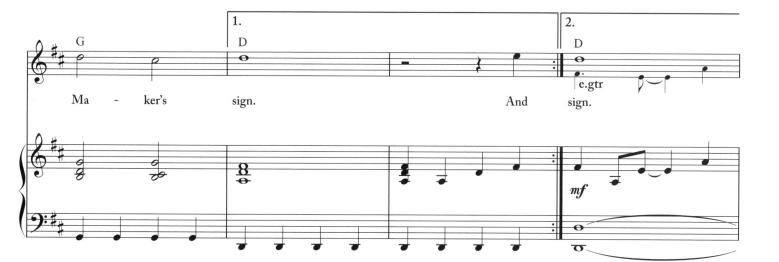

Ma - ker's sign. And sign.

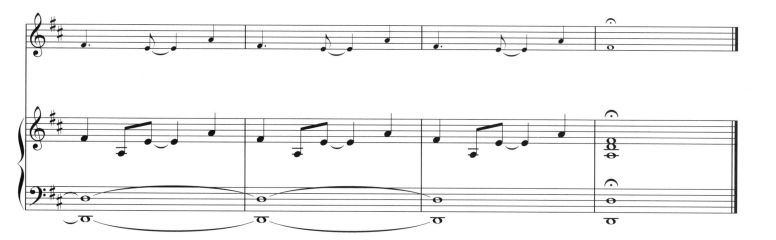

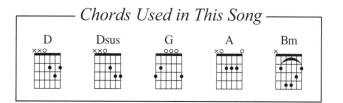

Chords Used in This Song

D   Dsus   G   A   Bm

My Heart Is Overwhelmed

Words and Music by
DYLAN THOMAS

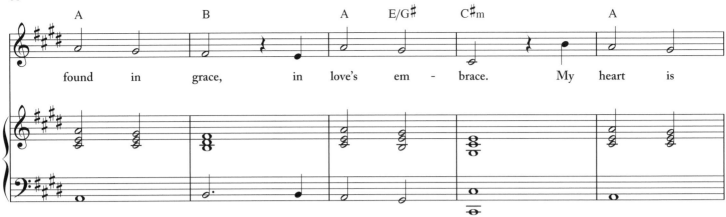

found in grace, in love's em - brace. My heart is

o - ver - whelmed. ___

cresc.

VERSE 2

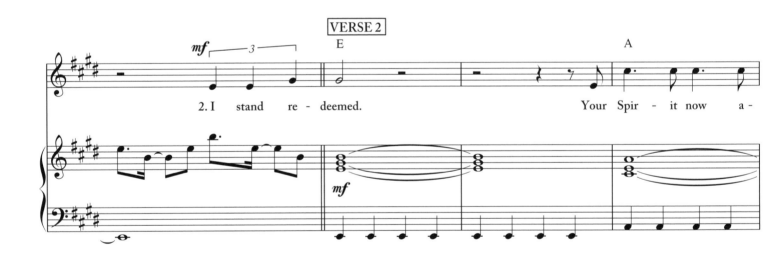

2. I stand re - deemed. Your Spir - it now a -

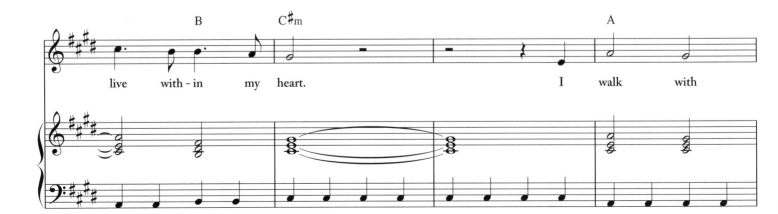

live with - in my heart. I walk with

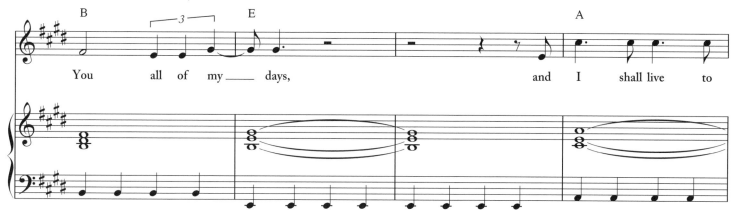

You all of my ____ days, and I shall live to

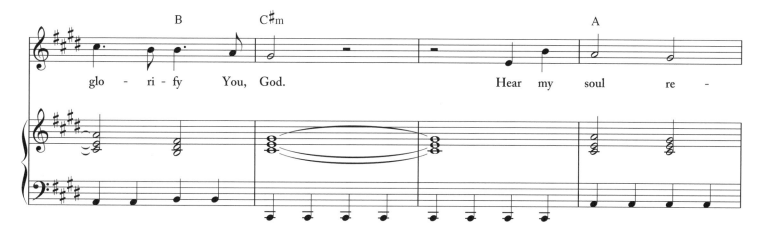

glo - ri - fy You, God. Hear my soul re -

CHORUS 2

joice. Your love has set the bro - ken cap - tives free.

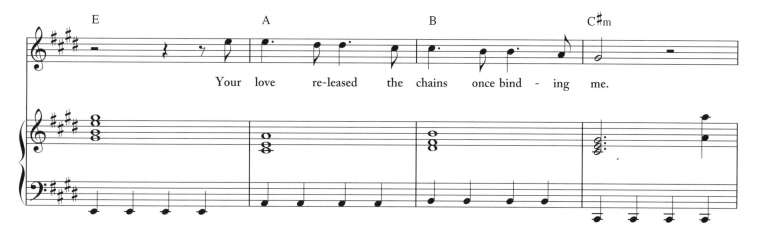

Your love re-leased the chains once bind - ing me.

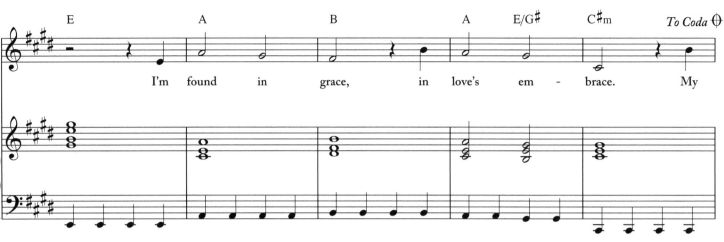

I'm found in grace, in love's em - brace. My

heart is o - ver - whelmed. __

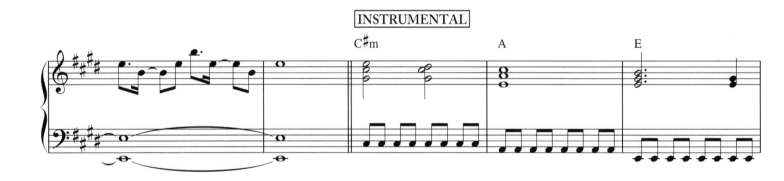

INSTRUMENTAL

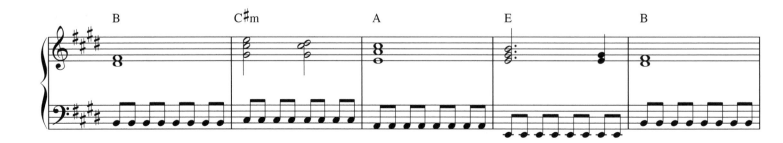

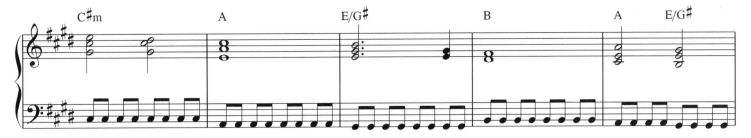

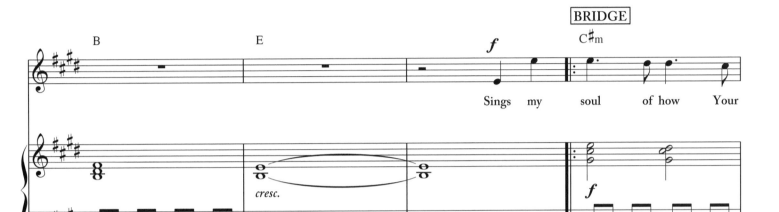

BRIDGE

Sings my soul of how Your

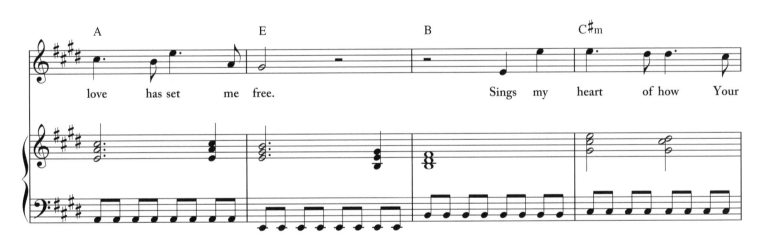

love has set me free. Sings my heart of how Your

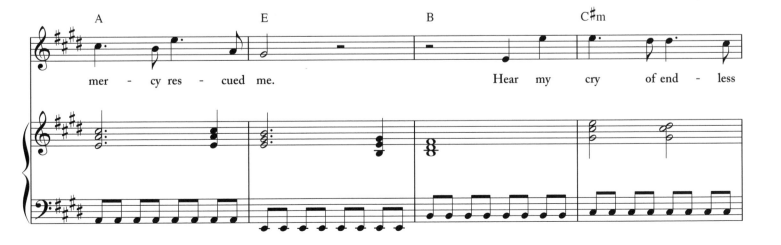

mer - cy res - cued me. Hear my cry of end - less

love, to my Sav-iour and ___ to my King. My heart is

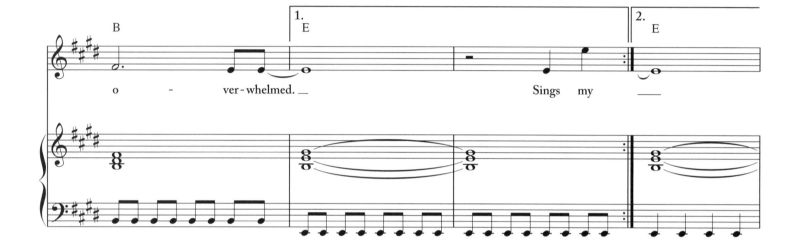

o - ver-whelmed. ___ Sings my ___

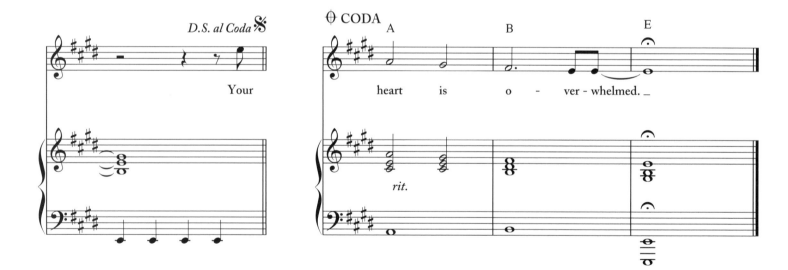

Your heart is o - ver - whelmed. ___

Chords Used in This Song

Cry of the Broken

Words and Music by
DARLENE ZSCHECH

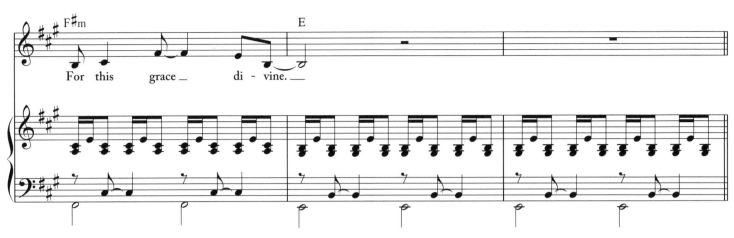

For this grace _ di - vine. _

VERSE 2, 3

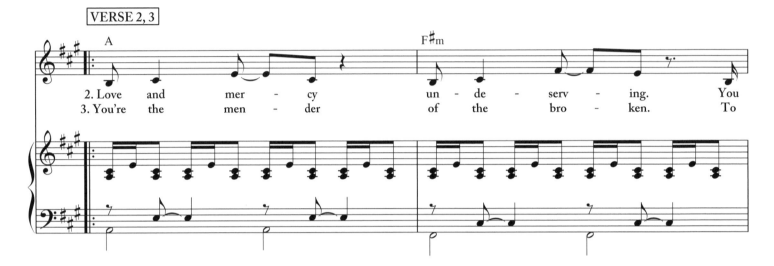

2. Love and mer - cy un - de - serv - ing. You
3. You're the men - der of the bro - ken. To

gave it all, _ the great - est sac - ri - fice. _
ev - 'ry out - cast, a friend and com - fort - er. _

You were wound -
I come bold -

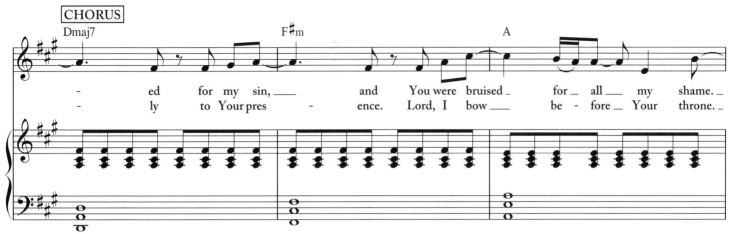

CHORUS

-ed for my sin, ____ and You were bruised ___ for ___ all ___ my shame. ___
-ly to Your pres - ence. Lord, I bow ___ be - fore ___ Your throne. ___

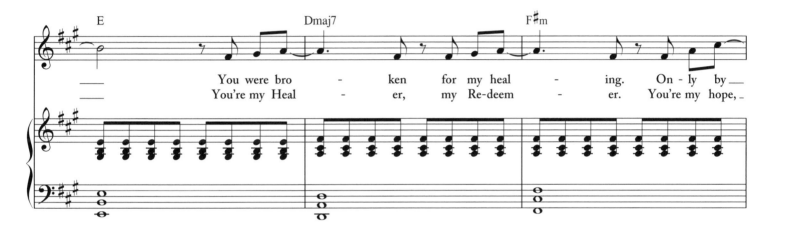

You were bro - ken for my heal - ing. On - ly by ___
You're my Heal - er, my Re-deem - er. You're my hope, ___

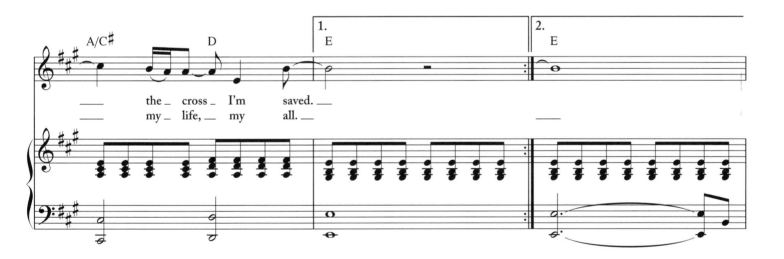

____ the ___ cross ___ I'm saved. ___
____ my ___ life, ___ my all. ___

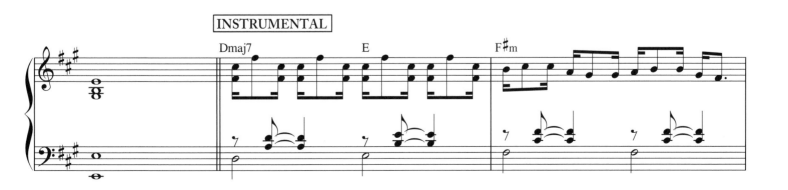

INSTRUMENTAL

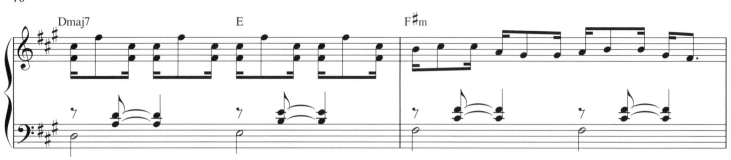

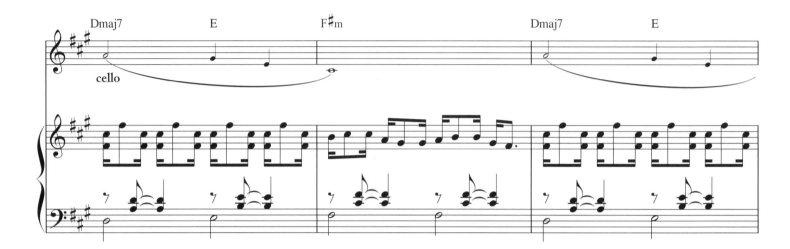

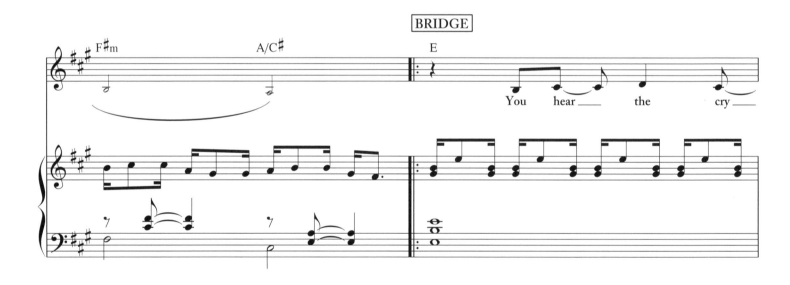

BRIDGE

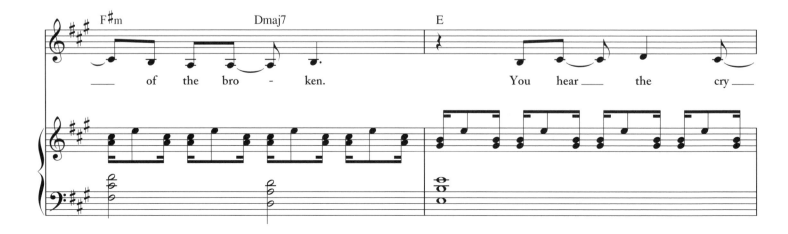

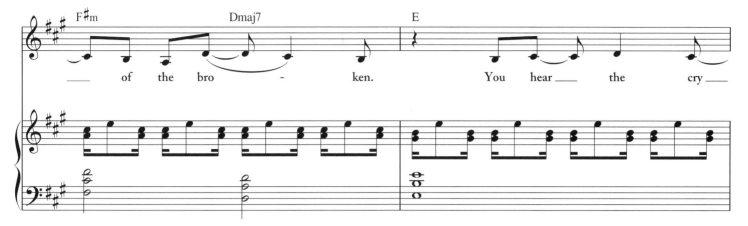

of the bro - ken. You hear ___ the cry ___

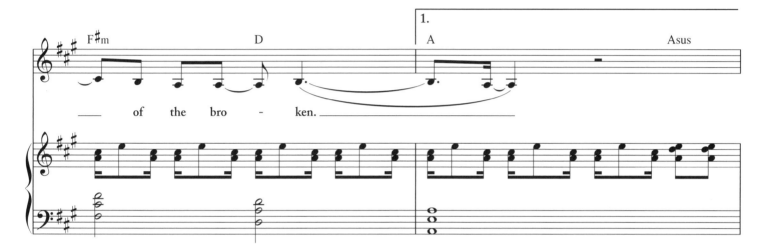

of the bro - ken. ___

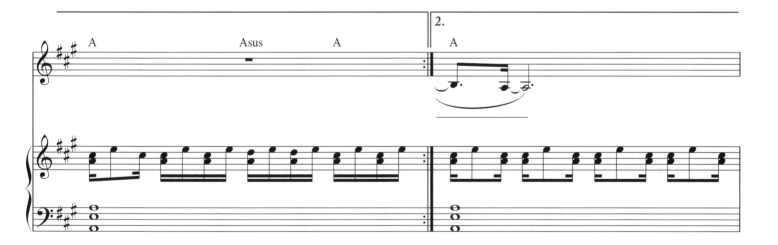

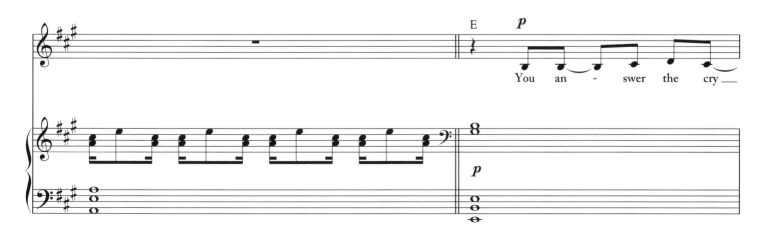

You an - swer the cry ___

78

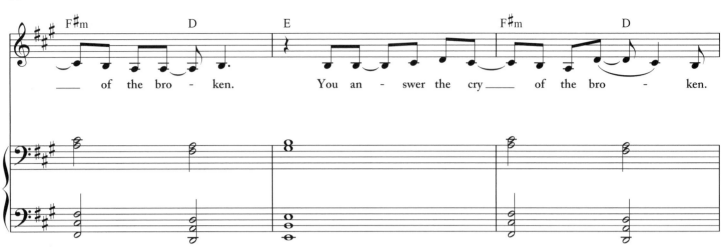

of the bro - ken. You an - swer the cry___ of the bro - ken.

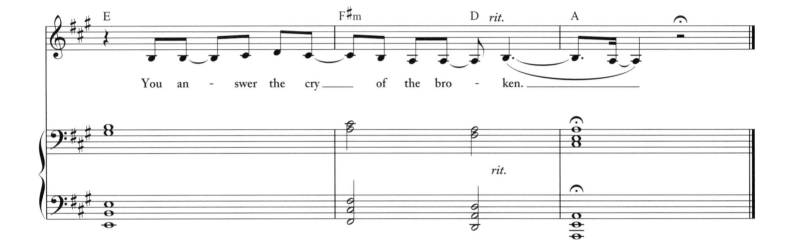

You an - swer the cry___ of the bro - ken.___

Chords Used in This Song

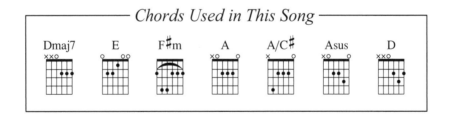

Dmaj7   E   F#m   A   A/C#   Asus   D